About This Resource

Why is this topic important?

More than ever, issues dealing with collaboration, trust, and ethical decision making are in the forefront of today's concerns and likely will continue to play a significant role well into the future. However, many find it difficult to master ethics and collaboration because these are often counter-intuitive behaviors that need to be practiced and nurtured. It is essential, therefore, for people to understand how individual choices that reflect cooperation and competition make an impact on both business and personal interactions, as well as the outcomes that result from the decisions made. Individuals must be proactive in these pursuits if they are to rely on integrity and cooperation for reaching their objectives more efficiently and effectively.

What can you achieve with this activity?

Based on the classic prisoner's dilemma, this simulation game is designed to create an awareness of the consequences of individual choices in terms of collaboration and ethics. The game puts into play the effects of competitive behavior on the possibilities for cooperation. It looks at the importance of trust and how it can be lost—particularly the fact that trust is relational and that it is affected by what happens between people or groups, and not simply by what one side does. The game also provides a very effective method of teaching ethics because the effects of one's actions can be related to fundamental principles of cooperation and competition.

Rather than simply hearing about the importance of ethical conduct, participants can see, based on their own actions, the implications of their behavior and the relevance of ethics in decision making. It motivates individuals to consider the consequences of ethical issues in terms of risk to themselves as well as to the collective group. Indeed, an important part of ethical training involves learning how individual actions affect others, especially when there is a conflict between the interests of the individuals and the interests of society.

How is this activity organized?

This simulation game consists of two components: The *Leader's Guide* provides background information on the prisoner's dilemma game structure, an overview of the *What Would You Do?* game, facilitator processing notes, debriefing questions with discussion notes on a variety of topics, and suggested learning extensions. The *Participant Workbook* contains the eight scenarios and accompanying scoring tables comprising the game, as well as the final scoring sheet and applied learning pages. Each participant will need one workbook.

About Pfeiffer

Pfeiffer serves the professional development and hands-on resource needs of training and human resource practitioners and gives them products to do their jobs better. We deliver proven ideas and solutions from experts in HR development and HR management, and we offer effective and customizable tools to improve workplace performance. From novice to seasoned professional, Pfeiffer is the source you can trust to make yourself and your organization more successful.

Essential Knowledge Pfeiffer produces insightful, practical, and comprehensive materials on topics that matter the most to training and HR professionals. Our Essential Knowledge resources translate the expertise of seasoned professionals into practical, how-to guidance on critical workplace issues and problems. These resources are supported by case studies, worksheets, and job aids and are frequently supplemented with CD-ROMs, websites, and other means of making the content easier to read, understand, and use.

Essential Tools Pfeiffer's Essential Tools resources save time and expense by offering proven, ready-to-use materials—including exercises, activities, games, instruments, and assessments—for use during a training or team-learning event. These resources are frequently offered in looseleaf or CD-ROM format to facilitate copying and customization of the material.

Pfeiffer also recognizes the remarkable power of new technologies in expanding the reach and effectiveness of training. While e-hype has often created whizbang solutions in search of a problem, we are dedicated to bringing convenience and enhancements to proven training solutions. All our e-tools comply with rigorous functionality standards. The most appropriate technology wrapped around essential content yields the perfect solution for today's on-the-go trainers and human resource professionals.

Pfeiffer
www.pfeiffer.com

Essential resources for training and HR professionals

Pfeiffer™

Lorraine L. Ukens

What Would You Do?

A Game of Ethical and Moral Dilemma

LEADER'S GUIDE

BICENTENNIAL 1807 WILEY 2007 BICENTENNIAL

Published by Pfeiffer
A Wiley Imprint
989 Market Street, San Francisco, CA 94103-1741
www.pfeiffer.com

Wiley Bicentennial logo: Richard J. Pacifico

For additional copies/bulk purchases of this book in the U.S. please contact 800-274-4434.

Pfeiffer books and products are available through most bookstores. To contact Pfeiffer directly call our Customer Care Department within the U.S. at 800-274-4434, outside the U.S. at 317-572-3985, fax 317-572-4002, or visit www.pfeiffer.com.

Pfeiffer also publishes its books in a variety of electronic formats. Some content that appears in print may not be available in electronic books.

ISBN: 978-0-7879-8537-0

Acquiring Editor: Martin Delahoussaye
Director of Development: Kathleen Dolan Davies
Developmental Editor: Susan Rachmeler
Production Editor: Michael Kay
Editor: Rebecca Taff
Editorial Assistant: Julie Rodriguez
Manufacturing Supervisor: Becky Morgan

Printed in the United States of America
Printing 10 9 8 7 6 5 4 3 2 1

Contents

Introduction

PURPOSE

We live in a fast-paced, turbulent world, in which each person is constantly faced with hard decisions to be made, both as an individual and as a member of a group. As pressures to succeed rise, more people are willing to risk doing things that are not entirely honest. Society emphasizes obtaining goals, and sometimes the end results become more important than how you go about doing things. There are numerous examples of unethical behavior broadcast in today's news media: athletes bulking up with steroids, students e-mailing test answers, people cheating on their taxes, land speculators scamming prospective buyers, politicians taking bribes or making behind-the-scenes deals. The list goes on and on. And it is not uncommon for these actions to be rewarded, or at least ignored.

When we see others cheat or act in an unethical way, it can lower personal inhibitions, and soon cheating doesn't seem so bad. So it is important to see how personal behaviors have an impact on others, whether they are members of a work or social group, an organization, a community, or even society as a whole. A major consideration in this analysis involves one's choice to compete against others for personal gain or to cooperate with others to create a synergy that obtains the best results for the group.

Based on the classic study in competition versus cooperation known as the "prisoner's dilemma," this simulation game is designed to provide a hands-on experience for examining the consequences of individual choices in terms of collaboration and ethics. This concept is extended to team actions because each individual member of the group is accountable for what the group does as a unit. The game is designed to help participants recognize the consequences of their actions on themselves and on others, while exploring the issues of risk taking and trust building in social interactions. Exploring these issues helps individuals make better choices and work in partnership with others to achieve the best overall results for all stakeholders.

AUDIENCE

The audience is all-inclusive because of the wide range of usage in terms of interpersonal relationships and ethical decision making. The game is especially suited for group members who are working toward establishing collaborative relationships or who want to explore ethical behavior in situations characterized by a conflict between individual and group interests. It is highly recommended for use in business, non-profit, and government organizations, as well as in academic settings, to explore issues involving the outcomes of competition versus cooperation and in discussing ethical standards.

HOW THIS RESOURCE IS ORGANIZED

This simulation game is based on the well-known prisoner's dilemma structure whereby participants must choose among options reflecting either cooperation or competition. The game consists of eight separate scenarios in which players select and then compare action choices with one another. These situations include a version of the original prisoner's dilemma, followed by seven additional dilemmas that escalate in terms of ethical decisions to be considered. The selection process for each scenario is repeated for several rounds, with and without communication between the players.

The *Leader's Guide* includes background information on the classic prisoner's dilemma; an overview of the *What Would You Do?* game and scoring information; facilitator guidelines; detailed step-by-step processing notes; debriefing questions and discussion notes; learning extensions; a Response Cards Sheet; and handouts on the topics of collaboration and ethics. The *Participant Workbook* includes an introduction to playing the game, the eight scenarios with accompanying scoring and response charts, the Final Scoring Sheet, and discussion and learning application pages.

KEY TERMS

Collaboration—the ability to work together to produce an integrated joint effort

Competition—an act that maximizes self-interest

Cooperation—an act that maximizes the interests of all parties involved (as individuals or as a collective)

Dilemma—a situation or state of perplexity that requires a choice between equally unfavorable options

Ethics—the study of the rules, standards, or principles that help determine whether an action is right or wrong

Game—the interaction or exchange between two or more players whereby each tries to win by choosing the best move, dependent on the other's response

Game theory—a mathematical method of decision making in which a competitive situation is analyzed to determine the optimal course of action for an interested party

Non-zero-sum game—a non-strictly competitive game in which there is no universally accepted solution; players have some complementary interests and some interests that are completely opposed

Risk—the potential harm that may arise from some present process or from some future event

Simulation game—a game that employs a situation depicting some aspect of reality for testing hypotheses in a "what if" analysis

Stakeholder—one who has a share or interest in an activity

Synergy—the effect of two or more agents working together to produce an effect greater than the sum of the parts

Tit-for-tat strategy—an approach in which one party cooperates on the first move of a game and then copies an opponent's last move for all subsequent moves

Trust—confidence in the integrity, ability, character, and truth of an individual or process

Zero-sum game—a competitive game in which the amount of "winnable resources" is fixed; what one player gains (positive) equals what the other player loses (negative) and the sum of the two is zero

Background on the Prisoner's Dilemma

The prisoner's dilemma is one of the earliest games developed in game theory, a branch of study that enables one to analyze behavior when individuals can make choices that give them some control—but not complete control—over what happens to them. The puzzle has attracted widespread attention in a variety of disciplines because of the many social interactions exhibited by the structure of the prisoner's dilemma. It illustrates a conflict between individual and group interests. The common occurrence of such circumstances in our lives makes the game structure a powerful tool for understanding behavior, especially in terms of cooperation and competition.

Additionally, the prisoner's dilemma structure naturally lends itself to issues concerning ethical choices. Participants are more likely to realize the importance of ethics in decision making when they can see the results of both ethical and unethical conduct. Activities that utilize this structure provide an effective method of teaching ethics because individual actions are clearly described within the scenarios.

To gain a better understanding of the prisoner's dilemma game and its basic structure, it is necessary to first take a look at the basic concept of game theory.

GAME THEORY

A game is an interaction or exchange between two or more players during which each tries to win by choosing the best move, dependent on the other's response.

Components of a game include players, strategies, actions, payoffs, outcomes, and equilibrium. A common distinction between game types is zero-sum and non-zero-sum.

Zero-sum games occur when the amount of winnable resources is fixed. What is gained by one player is lost by another. In other words, the sum of what is gained (positive) and what is lost (negative) equals zero. This corresponds to a condition of pure competition. Simply put, I win and you lose (or vice versa!). This means that an optimal solution always can be found—at least for one player. Most games that people play for recreation are zero-sum. However, this condition generally does not represent the conflicts faced in the real world because problems do not usually have such straightforward results.

Non-zero-sum games reflect the dynamics of the world in which we live because they do not have universally accepted solutions or predictable outcomes. In these games, the total amount to be gained is variable, so both players can win (or lose). They contain elements of both competition and cooperation because players have some interests that are complementary and some that are completely opposed. When players are able to gain something by collaborating in some way, they can create a synergy to benefit everyone. For example, a business contract ideally is a positive-sum game, where each side is better off than if they didn't have the contract.

Game theory examines how decisions are made in situations in which strategic interaction (moves and countermoves) occurs between rivals. It provides ways to evaluate the most favorable behavior for parties involved in situations in which individual interests conflict with one another. This look at decision making under conditions of uncertainty and interdependence can be applied to a wide range of situations, including social interactions, economics, commerce, politics, and even the military.

GAME STRUCTURE

The prisoner's dilemma is only one of many illustrative examples of the logical reasoning and complex decisions involved in game theory. Puzzles with this structure were developed in 1950 at the RAND Corporation, a major center for the development of game theory. They were used to illustrate the failure of using lowest-risk strategies and the potential for conflict between individual and group interests. The title "Prisoner's Dilemma" and the version with prison sentences as payoffs are due to Albert Tucker, who wanted to make the idea more accessible to an audience of Stanford psychologists.

The game is an excellent way to examine both collaboration and ethical decision making because there is not just one favorable strategy, and opposing parties must rely on one another to achieve more favorable results. As a non-zero-sum game that is very broad in application, its social dilemma structure makes it especially useful for exploring problems of cooperation as well as moral and ethical situations.

Since any relationship with two (or more) parties can imply such a dilemma, the game helps us understand what governs the balance between cooperation and competition in business, in politics, and in social settings. The situation involves two people who must separately make decisions with consequences not only for their own selves, but also for one another. What makes the prisoner's dilemma such a fascinating game is that the optimal outcome, the one that would be best for all players, is not always the one an individual player will reach. However, when the game is played repeatedly, chances improve for such a result to happen.

THE SCENARIO

The dilemma owes its name to the scenario in which two people suspected of a burglary are arrested in the course of committing some minor offense. In the classic game, the pair is separated and interrogated, and each is given the choice of confessing to the crime and implicating the other, or remaining silent. If both confess, each will spend only a few years in prison. If both remain silent, they receive an even lighter sentence. However, if only one confesses and the other does not, the one who confessed is rewarded by being set free, while the other one receives a long jail term.

The dilemma arises when it is assumed that both prisoners only care about minimizing their own jail terms. The cooperative option between the two is to remain silent, while the individualistic or competitive option is to confess (that is, "defect"). However, neither prisoner knows the choice of his accomplice. Even if they were able to talk to one another, neither could be sure the other could be trusted.

Most of us don't find ourselves in exactly this position, but the prisoner's dilemma scenario provides a logical structure for many other circumstances we do face every day in real life. Whether we compete with others in business or in our personal lives, our choices can often be phrased in terms of the prisoner's dilemma. The parties involved generally will be better off working together if each resists the temptation to go it alone and instead cooperates with or remains loyal to the other(s). Generally, when each party pursues its own interests exclusively, the situation will lead to a worse outcome overall than if they cooperated.

GAME STRATEGY

Whenever an individual interacts with a group (two or more people), a dilemma generally arises having characteristics of the prisoner's dilemma in which a rational choice (that is, taking the action that best serves your personal interest) produces an inferior result. The idea is that each player gains when both cooperate; however, if only one of them cooperates, the other one, who competes, will gain more. If both parties compete, both lose (or at the least gain very little) but not as much as the "cheated" player whose cooperation is not returned. (See Payoff Matrix on the next page.)

The strategy of competition is considered a dominating strategy because it yields a better outcome for a player, regardless of what the other person does. But where the dominating strategy is rational for the individual, an even more optimal result may be gained through a cooperative strategy. Using the classic prisoner's dilemma as an example, the prisoners receive the lowest sentence if both are motivated not to confess by trusting one another to remain loyal. In order to achieve such an outcome, both players must have an agreement that can be reasonably enforced and sufficient trust in one another. If one is motivated to cheat on the agreement or betray that loyalty, this uncooperative move can undermine any cooperative strategies. This is why knowledge is absolutely essential to making an individually optimal decision.

The best strategy for maximizing points for any one individual is to select a competitive option. However, if both players follow this line of reasoning, they end up worse off than if both had cooperated. Cooperating does not give an individual the best possible outcome, but it will obtain a better result than either individual could achieve if both parties choose to compete.

People confront a dilemma concerning their decisions because, when motivated solely by self-interest, they face more severe consequences than when motivated by group interests. In order to make the best choice, each player would have to presume to know what the other will do, but this information is only available if the game is played again and again. With repeated play, the optimal strategy becomes dependent on each of the preceding choices made by the other player. Playing the game for a defined number of times would make the rational choice for each player to compete on the last move because there is no chance for retaliation. However, if there is an experience of cooperation in earlier rounds of the game, trust can build between players and the choice for competition may be reduced. This positive behavior is most evident if the group is small, which in turn encourages individuals within the group to continue to cooperate. With this in mind, the prisoner's dilemma game allows for the possibility that cooperation can evolve in the long run, even though in the short run it seems better to compete.

PAYOFF MATRIX

The payoff matrix is structured for individual self-interest to be more rewarding to the individual. However, in the long run, if two individuals both cooperate, no one person loses. The point assignments for the various payoffs can be generalized for use with any scenario as long as the Temptation to compete is greater than the Reward for mutual cooperation, which is greater than the Punishment for both parties to compete, with the worst option being the "Sucker's Payoff" to the party who decides to cooperate when the other party competes (T > R > P > S).

	Cooperate	Compete
Cooperate	win/win	lose much/win much
Compete	win much/lose much	lose/lose

The predicament faced by players in the prisoner's dilemma is that the highest reward is for an individual to compete. But the outcome obtained when both players compete is worse for each individual than the outcome they would have obtained had both cooperated. Therefore, the puzzle illustrates a conflict between individual and group rationality. A group whose members pursue their own self-interests may individually all end up worse off than those members who act in the best interest of the group.

TIT-FOR-TAT STRATEGY

When playing the game repeatedly, most studies concluded that the most successful strategy was something called "tit for tat." This strategy has three characteristics that account for its impressive performance: (1) nice, in which a person cooperates on the first move; (2) retaliatory, in which a person chooses competition to punish the other player's prior competitive move; and (3) forgiving, where a person immediately returns to cooperation after one cooperative move by an adversary.

Punishment won't work unless cheating by another player can be detected. Tit-for-tat theory states you will likely cheat if, and only if, your rival cheated in the previous round. However, should a rival's innocent actions be misinterpreted as cheating, then tit for tat runs the risk of setting off successive rounds of unwarranted retaliation. If the individuals repeatedly interact with one another over a long period of time, the prospect of future cooperation may keep them from cheating on one another.

FACTORS

Several factors affect the outcome of the prisoner's dilemma. The three most significant ones are described below.

Repeated Play

The number of times the game is played is an important factor. If the game were played only once, players would not have to fear retaliation from their opponents, so they may play differently than they would in a game played repeatedly. Repetition provides a chance for cooperation because players know interaction will occur again. Therefore, trust for the other player must be built up, based on past performance. The way in which individuals deal with conflicts of interest, especially when individual interests conflict with their duties to others, is at the heart of what ethical theory is expected to resolve. In the prisoner's dilemma, as in the real world, the temptation to compete is lower when the interactions are perceived to be ongoing rather than having an end. Therefore, when a relationship is considered to be long-term, the assessment of the association is generally more positive. Past history of the interactions with other players influences current decisions.

Trust

Another key factor in the prisoner's dilemma is the importance of trust. It is crucial to believe it when both partners assure one another they will cooperate. After all, if you suspect your partner may renege on the deal, then you're better off repaying his cheating with cheating. What's more, your suspicions are hardly unfounded, since your partner does have a temptation to cheat because that choice results in the highest individual payoff. Unethical behavior, while apparently rewarding to the individual because the unethical person does relatively better than the ethical players, is ultimately self-defeating because of the feedback effect such behavior has on the individual. This unethical conduct not only harms the group, but it also adversely affects the individual engaged in the questionable activity in terms of trust and worth.

Communication

Communication is also an important aspect of the game. If two players cannot communicate with one another, and each behaves to promote a rational self-interest, it is almost certain both will do worse as a result. One striking thing about cooperation is that it can occur *without* the players being allowed to converse. The reason this could happen is that the same players would interact several times. So, by observing what a particular player did on the last occasion, the other player could gather information about expected future behavior. This is, in a sense, a type of communication—and certainly a form of information transmission. What's more, players could "punish" one another for past cheating and reward one another for past cooperation.

IMPLICATIONS

The prisoner's dilemma presents a case in which actions determined by self-interest are not in the group's interest. However, the game can be generalized to any scenario in which two or more players are in a conflict situation when the best situation is for both to cooperate, but the worst individual outcome is to be a player who cooperates when the other one competes.

Overview of *What Would You Do?* Game

This *Leader's Guide* contains the step-by-step instructions for running the game, which can be found in the Processing Notes. The discussion questions and response notes are located in the Debriefing section that follows. The questions cover actions specific to the play of the game, as well as topics that can be applied to the issues of cooperation and ethics. Each question referring to the game process is accompanied by notes to help guide the discussion. The facilitator should have a working knowledge of the prisoner's dilemma game structure and its implications. Participant handouts on the topics of collaboration and ethics are included at the end of this Guide. The information also may be helpful to the facilitator when conducting the application discussion.

The *Participant Workbook* contains an introductory section on Playing the Game that explains the rules, how to play a round, and sample scoring. The game itself begins with a version of the classic prisoner's dilemma in which participants must make choices reflecting cooperation (group interest) or competition (self-interest). The remaining seven scenarios present moral and ethical dilemmas requiring participants to make choices from among ethical (cooperative) and unethical (competitive) options.

PLAYING THE GAME

Participants are given the goal of individually scoring the highest number of points at the end of the game. They will work in pairs, then in sets of two teams, and finally in a set of three teams. Teams will be comprised of four or five members each. Each of the eight scenarios requires five rounds of decision making, with discussion only permitted for the last five situations.

The decision-making process requires the player to select a card with the letter A or B to correspond to the two possible actions presented for any one situation. These selections indicate a cooperative (ethical) choice for A and a competitive (unethical) choice for B. For each round, the participants playing one another will keep their cards concealed until each has made a selection, revealing the cards at the same time. By laying the cards face down, the possibility of a player knowing the other player's selection in advance is eliminated. A scoring chart accompanies each scenario, with the payoff schedule for the various card combinations.

Participants will record points in their individual workbooks for each round of play to reflect the appropriate card combination found in the scoring chart for each scenario. When the players have completed five rounds and a score has been calculated, all participants will be directed to turn to the next scenario. This process will be continued for all of the scenarios, and a final tally of the eight scores will be calculated to determine the winner.

GAME DESIGN

In framing the scenarios as prisoner's dilemma games, "ethical" can be interpreted to mean "balancing other's welfare with your own" while being "unethical" means "acting without regard to others." The dilemmas build in ethical considerations, testing an individual's choice against one other player, and then as part of a team in which all members must attempt to agree on an option to play against other groups.

Variables

The following factors were controlled in the game design to create varying conditions that would lead to exploration of issues related to collaboration and ethics. The chart on the next page provides a snapshot of these variables, which are explained in more detail below.

Scenario	Players	Play	Discussion	Stakeholders	Payoff
1	2 individuals	3 min.	No	Individual	Punishment
2	2 individuals	3 min.	No	Individual	Punishment
3	2 individuals	3 min.	No	Individual/ Organization	Punishment
4	2 individuals	6 min.	Yes	Individual/ Organization	Punishment
5	2 individuals	6 min.	Yes	Individual/ Group/ Organization	Punishment
6	2 teams	12 min.	Yes	Individual/ Community	Reward
7	2 teams	12 min.	Yes	Individual/ Organization/ Society	Reward
8	3 teams	15 min.	Yes	Organization/ Society	Reward

Players

Play initially occurs with a pair of individuals as "opponents" during the first five scenarios. In the later ones, it switches to collective play wherein team members must work together to arrive at group decisions to be played against the opposing team. This allows an exploration of the complexities of achieving collaboration as the number of players grows. Applying this to ethical decision making, participants can see the impact that individual actions have on other stakeholders. In addition, issues of trust building can be examined by comparing actions taken between the pairs as play progressed and then when opponents become team members.

Time Limits

The play runs quickly in the first rounds, since these involve individual choices that are limited by no verbal communication. When the discussion periods are introduced, they are limited to introduce a sense of time pressure. As the number of players involved in the discussions grows, the amount of time also is increased to allow for the extended lines of communication.

Communication

Verbal communication is not allowed between opposing players during the first three scenarios to provide a baseline for later comparisons when it is allowed. Each of the last five situations allows one brief discussion period for players (as individuals or teams) between the third and fourth rounds of play. This provides a condition to explore various aspects of communication when working with others, either as an individual or as a group. Since players may begin to negotiate plays during the discussions, it is possible to look at the role of influence and issues of trust both within and across groups.

Stakeholders

A stakeholder is someone who has a share or interest in an activity that occurs. In this game, there is an escalation in the scope of the parties who are affected by the decision made in each scenario. The consequence options presented in the situations begin to move from a focus on personal interests to the ramification of how others are being affected by a decision. These other stakeholders range from the larger group (department) or organization to the community or society as a whole. By increasing the stakes that a personal decision will affect others, the scenarios present participants with the opportunity to use higher-level decision-making skills and assess the amount of risk they are willing to take.

Motivation

The scoring chart used for the first five scenarios contains negative payoffs intended to create an appearance of "punishment," while the last three have generally positive payoffs (zero is the worst you can score) so as to generate a sense of "reward" for the outcome of one's action. This design allows for an examination of what incentives motivate a person to act in a certain situation. It is important to remember, however, that these payoffs occur as a result of the relationship of the actions of both opponents. Therefore, individual motivation should be examined within the context of how one's actions are perceived by others and the extent to which personal decisions have implications outside of oneself.

The Payoffs

The points assigned to the various card combinations were determined using the payoff equation from the classic prisoner's dilemma study. This means that the gain for mutual cooperation is always kept smaller than the gain for one-sided competition, so there is always a temptation for the individual to compete or act unethically. As stated previously, the equation is such that the Temptation to compete is greater than the Reward for mutual cooperation, which is greater than the Punishment if all players compete, while the "Sucker's Payoff" is the worst option for a player. It is important to note that the outcome options do not need to be proportionately equal for any particular scenario, but merely balanced in relationship to this equation.

The original game was designed for interaction between two players with a payoff matrix containing four choices. However, the concept can be extended to interactions with more players. For three players, each one would need to weigh possible outcomes of cooperation and competition with two counterparts. This would result in a three-dimensional matrix with eight possibilities. However, for the three-team situation presented here, the scoring matrix was designed to account for the choice made by Team 1 in combination with Team 2 **or** Team 3, rather than including separate options for both of the additional players. Using this approach means there are six possible consequences for Scenario 8.

IMPLICATIONS

This simulation game shows that there are implications to one's actions. Based on the original prisoner's dilemma game structure, it provides a hands-on examination of how one's behavior affects others in relation to a variety of conditions. If both players choose to compete, they each end up with a payoff that is inferior to the reward they would receive if they had cooperated. Even though competition is individually optimal, it is not in the collective interest of the players to compete. If both players give up individual interests and choose to cooperate, both will receive a greater outcome than they would earn by both competing.

In terms of moral decision making, unethical behavior (competition) can harm others in the sense that they may be made worse off by the unethical conduct of an individual. Thinking and acting ethically involves a realization of how one's actions affect others, especially when there is a conflict between immediate personal interest and the interest of others. This illustrates the important point that unethical behavior is frequently self-defeating because it produces an outcome everyone agrees is individually and collectively inferior to that realized under ethical or cooperative behavior.

Social dilemma games provide an interesting and effective method of introducing questions and of generating discussions of ethical issues and principles. The basic insight offered by examining these situations is that individual obligations to consider the social welfare of the group require decision makers to rise above their own narrow self-interests.

The application to business ethics is clear. Ethical business leaders consider the ramifications of the decisions they make. By examining the implications of self-interested behavior in the context of the prisoner's dilemma, ethics training can help illustrate how business decisions affect others and how one's environment affects the incentives to cooperate with or take advantage of others.

There is no single "right" solution to the dilemmas presented. The ethically defined situations merely provide a way for participants to explore how individual actions have consequences not only for oneself but for other stakeholders as well, in terms of both collaboration and ethical considerations. A fundamental insight gained from analyzing the game is that an adherence to ethical principles can result in greater group *and* individual rewards, but only if players pass up the individual incentive to take advantage of one another through strictly competitive or unethical actions.

Facilitator Guidelines

The role of the facilitator is to guide participants in the process of inquiry and analysis to help them make the connection between the activity and the intent of the learning. Therefore, it is important for the activity to be set up, run, and discussed properly with a tie back to the real world.

- Before conducting the game, the facilitator should be thoroughly familiar with the background information, game structure, the payoff scoring matrix designs, and the discussion notes provided in the Debriefing section.
- During the play of the game, if **all** players appear to have completed a timed task, proceed to the next step even if the noted time limits have not lapsed. This will help the game to move along and will keep the participants engaged.
- The debriefing session is the most important aspect of any simulation, as it allows participants to reflect on the lessons learned from an amusing game-like environment. It is important to allow sufficient time for this reflection and application process to occur.
- A critical part of the learning process is real-world application. Participants should be encouraged to use the insights gained during play by examining ways to create positive behavior change in real-world situations, using the Learning Insights and Action Planning sheets in the *Participant Workbook*.

- The purpose of the game is to explore the process and not necessarily analyze the content of the scenarios. You may choose to examine the topic of ethics in more depth by conducting follow-up sessions, and several suggestions have been provided at the end of the Debriefing section under Learning Extensions.

Processing Notes

GOALS

- To choose action steps for ethical dilemmas in which a conflict exists between individual and group interests.
- To explore consequences of cooperation and competition.
- To experience the implications of trust building and trust betrayal.
- To discuss the ethical ramifications and risk levels of personal decisions.
- To explore the role of communication in the decision-making process.

GROUP SIZE

Twelve to forty-five participants, who will work in pairs and in sets of two, then in three teams of four or five persons each.

TIME REQUIRED

Approximately three hours, as follows:

- Instructions, Play, and Scoring—90 minutes
- Break—15 minutes
- Debriefing Discussions—60 minutes
- Reflection and Action Planning—15 minutes

MATERIALS

- A *What Would You Do? Participant Workbook* for each participant.
- Copies of Handout 1 and Handout 2 for all participants.
- A pencil or pen for each participant.
- A pair of Response Cards (A and B) for each participant.
- A prize for the winner.
- A clock or timer to monitor play.
- A flip chart and felt-tipped markers for the facilitator.
- Paper and pen for observer, if necessary.

PHYSICAL SETTING

A room large enough for the entire group, with sufficient space for subgroups of up to five participants to meet together simultaneously without distracting one another.

PREPARATION

- Duplicate one copy of each of the two Handouts for every participant.
- Duplicate the Response Cards Sheet on card stock and cut into individual cards. Prepare enough sets of cards A and B to accommodate all participants.
- Familiarize yourself with the information provided in the sections titled "Background of the Prisoner's Dilemma" and "Overview of What Would You Do? Game." In addition, it is recommended that you review the two participant Handouts for guidance in facilitating the debriefing discussion.

PROCESS

1. Randomly assign participants to work in pairs, with each pair located in close proximity to one another but separated from other pairs in the room. [*NOTE:* If there are an odd number of participants, invite one individual to become a neutral observer during the game. Provide the participant with paper and pen and ask that comments be recorded on the interactions that occur throughout the exercise.]
2. Distribute a copy of the *Participant Workbook*, a pencil or pen, and a pair of Response Cards (A and B) to each participant. Tell the participants that they are to proceed through the workbook only as directed.
3. Tell participants to open the workbook to page 1. Read aloud the information on Playing the Game and Directions for Playing a Round. Review the Sample Scoring and clarify any issues regarding the scoring process.
4. Tell participants to turn to Scenario 1 on page 3. Read aloud the scenario and the instructions. Emphasize that participants should refrain

from turning to the next scenario until directed to do so and that pairs are not to discuss the game if they finish before other pairs. Announce that participants are to begin. Allow approximately three minutes for play and scoring, stopping the game when all pairs appear to have completed the assignment.

5. Tell participants to turn to Scenario 2 on page 5. Read aloud the scenario and the instructions, emphasizing that participants are to refrain from turning to the next scenario until directed to do so and that they should not discuss the game if they finish before other pairs. Announce that the participants should begin. Allow approximately three minutes for play and scoring.
6. Tell participants to turn to Scenario 3 on page 7. Read aloud the scenario and the instructions. Emphasize that participants are to follow the restrictions stated. Announce that the participants should begin. Allow approximately three minutes for play and scoring.
7. Tell participants to turn to Scenario 4 on page 9. Read aloud the scenario, stressing that the other player represents *all other employees*, and the subsequent instructions. Announce for players to conduct Rounds 1 through 3, allowing approximately two minutes for play, giving a brief warning before time expires. At the end of this period, announce the intergroup discussion round and time it for two minutes. Announce the beginning of the period for Rounds 4 and 5 and scoring. Remind players to stop before going to the next scenario if they finish before other pairs. Allow approximately two additional minutes for play and scoring.
8. Tell participants to turn to Scenario 5 on page 11. Read aloud the scenario and the instructions. Announce for players to conduct Rounds 1 through 3, allowing approximately two minutes for play, giving a brief warning before time expires. At the end of this period, announce the intergroup discussion round and time it for two minutes. Announce the beginning of the period for Rounds 4 and 5 and scoring. Remind players to stop before going to the next scenario if they finish before other pairs. Allow approximately two additional minutes for play and scoring.
9. Explain that the rest of the game will be played in teams. Ask each pair of players to join with another pair to form a new team. [*NOTE:* If an odd number of groups form, assign members of the extra group

to other teams so that some consist of five players each.] Provide each team with a number and tell Teams 1 and 2 to form a set, Teams 3 and 4 to form a set, and so forth. Each set of two teams should meet in a separate area of the room to allow for privacy. Tell participants that only one set of Response Cards will be used per team and to set aside all additional sets. Stress that all members of a team will record the *same response* and receive the *same score* for the resulting card combination.

10. Tell participants to turn to Scenario 6 on page 13. Read aloud the scenario and the instructions. Announce that teams are to conduct Rounds 1 through 3, allowing approximately five minutes for play, giving a one-minute warning before time expires. At the end of this period, announce the intergroup discussion round and time it for two minutes. Ask participants to regroup with their team members. Announce the beginning of the period for Rounds 4 and 5 and scoring. Remind teams to stop before going to the next scenario if they finish before others. Allow approximately five minutes for play and scoring.

11. Tell participants to turn to Scenario 7 on page 15. Read aloud the scenario and the instructions. Announce for teams to conduct Rounds 1 through 3, allowing approximately five minutes for play, giving a one-minute warning before time expires. At the end of this period, announce the intergroup discussion round and time it for two minutes. Ask participants to regroup with their team members. Announce the beginning of the period for Rounds 4 and 5 and scoring. Remind teams to stop before going to the next scenario if they finish before others. Allow approximately five minutes for play and scoring.

12. Explain that the last scenario will involve playing the game in sets of three teams each. Randomly assign the participants to form new teams of three to five persons each, providing each group with a number. Direct Teams 1, 2, and 3 to work together; Teams 4, 5, and 6 to work together; and so forth. Instruct each set of three teams to work together in an area of the room that allows for privacy.

13. Tell participants to turn to Scenario 8 on page 17. Read aloud the scenario and the instructions. Announce for teams to conduct Rounds 1 through 3, allowing approximately five minutes for play, giving a one-minute warning before time expires. At the end of this period, announce the intergroup discussion round and time for five minutes. Ask participants to regroup with their team members. Announce the

beginning of the period for Rounds 4 and 5 and scoring. Remind teams to stop before going on if they finish before others. Allow approximately five minutes for play and scoring.

14. Tell participants to turn to page 19 for the Final Scoring Sheet. Read the instructions aloud and allow several minutes for individuals to record their scores and calculate the Final Score. Determine the individual with the highest score and award the prize. If there is a tie, no award is to be made.

15. Announce a fifteen-minute break for participants.

16. After the break, tell the participants to turn to the Small Group Discussion question on page 20. Ask them to write some comments in response to the question. Allow approximately three minutes for individual work, and then have participants stop. While remaining in the same teams, ask groups to discuss their comments. Allow approximately seven minutes and then stop the discussion.

17. Refer to the Debriefing section that follows to conduct a large group discussion (approximately forty-five minutes) using the questions and corresponding notes, then proceed to the instructions for Closing at the end of the section.

Debriefing

THE GAME PROCESS

NOTE: First ask that people refer to specific incidents that occurred during the game. Next, get them to look at the process, that is, how one action response led to another.

What overall strategy did you employ to achieve the highest score? Was it effective? Why or why not?

Initially, players may have chosen a competitive approach because of the presented and implied emphasis on winning. Most rational players will choose to compete because the payoff is more conducive to their self-interest. However, over the long term, the outcome consistently is better for the players to cooperate rather than to compete. This is true because the other player comes to the same conclusion as you when considering the win-lose possibilities. For example, in the initial scenarios, a player who competes will earn 10 points if the other cooperates (and who receives −10 points). Therefore, the net result creates a situation that is inferior when both parties compete rather than both cooperate. That is, in terms of scoring, both competing would earn 0 points as opposed to both cooperating, which would earn 5 points.

How did the scoring system affect the decisions you made?

There are conflicting goals presented to the players: Score the highest points to win, but do the right thing by acting in a cooperative or ethical way. The payoff scoring is structured for self-interest to be more rewarding to the individual. The highest scoring option is based on a temptation to compete, so this becomes the dominating strategy if you want to earn the most points. However, in the long run, it should become obvious that, if both players choose a cooperative option, no one person loses. Also, the scoring tables in the earlier scenarios presented negative scores, which might indicate "punishment" to some players. However, in later scenarios, the payoffs seem to take on a "reward" aspect because the worst card combination resulted in a neutral score (zero).

Achieving a high score implies a competitive approach. How did this goal affect your decision-making options during the game?

The issues generally involved are the amount of risk to take and the possibility of taking advantage of other players. Some players may have chosen to make a more risky, unethical selection to gain extra points. This would mean that the option chosen represented the dominating strategy of competition. If one player chose to be competitive, the other player may have retaliated in the ensuing rounds by making a competitive response. This repetitive behavior would only be broken if the players recognized that neither one was gaining points and instead decided to cooperate.

What made cooperation more difficult?

In the first three scenarios, the lack of communication was a major factor in hindering a player's ability to discuss mutually cooperative options. This meant that players had to interpret the intentions of the partners based on their impression of the person and his or her previous actions. Also, if another player repeatedly made competitive choices, it was more difficult to trust that person's motives in future moves. Individual perception and stereotyping could prevent a player from accurately interpreting the actions of another player. If moves were misinterpreted, retaliatory reactions could occur and trigger a series of competitive responses. All these factors have an impact on a player's ability to build trust with another player, a major determinant for collaborative efforts.

Did you feel you could trust the other players during the game? Why or why not?

Because there was no communication allowed in the beginning scenarios, it may have been difficult for one player to trust another. As the game progressed, the past performance of players may have set the tone for how an individual would make a decision. Trust is needed to move from a non-cooperative to a cooperative situation, and it is clearly related to some kind of belief in another's credibility. In order to resolve a social dilemma, it is necessary for a person to have accurate information about whether the other players will betray trust, or whether they will be trustworthy.

The better one knows the other player, the more likely it is that he or she will cooperate rather than compete because of the emotional connection that is gained through personal acquaintance. That is, the more entwined destinies are, the stronger the feeling is for working together, especially when it is in the interest of the group. Social values and norms in most cultures deem being trustworthy a positive trait. Being trusted is not only seen as beneficial on a personal level but it is perceived as critical for building and maintaining close relationships.

During the game, how did repeated play with the same person affect the way in which players treated one another? What happened when opponents formed a team whose members had to work together? What changes in group dynamics occurred when a third team was introduced in the play?

The fact that there were several rounds for each scenario afforded the players an indication of one another's styles of play based on past performance. As individuals interacted repeatedly, a stronger relationship in terms of trust and cooperation should have developed as play progressed. Research has shown that there is no real incentive for either player to do anything but compete when the length of the relationship between players is a short-term one.

Another factor is that the game is being played a known number of rounds. In such a situation, there is a good chance players will move toward competition on the last move. If this is the assumption, a player may be inclined to compete in an earlier round. If the game had been played an indefinite number of times, cooperation would generally evolve as the best policy. In the real world, if a relationship is repeated over a long period of time, the prospect of future cooperation may keep individuals from "cheating" on one another. This is a classic tit-for-tat strategy in which one party cooperates on the first move of a game and then copies an opponent's last move for the rest of the moves. This is the reason why long-term relationships generate more cooperative behavior than short-term ones.

How did the prior actions of players affect your personal choices as time went on?

Using a "tit-for-tat" strategy, the game is designed to reward cooperation and punish competition over repeated interactions. In essence, this means that, on your move, you do the exact same thing that the other player did on the prior move. There are actually three play movements for this type of strategy: (1) Nice, in which both players cooperate on the first move of the game; (2) Retaliatory, in which a player competes if an individual competed on the prior move; and (3) Forgiving, in which a player cooperates with a past competitor who now has chosen to cooperate. If players always chose to compete, it was hard to trust them in future moves. In the long run, the "nice" style of tit for tat is the best strategy; therefore, it pays to cooperate.

An important lesson in the game is that the better you know the other player, the more likely you will be to learn to cooperate. If you know that you will never have to meet with the other player again, the more likely it is that you will compete. If you will have to deal with the other player many more times, you will be more inclined to cooperate, even if it is only because of fear of retaliation.

How does individual perception influence expectations of another player's actions?

Individuals develop strategies for behavior based on their expectations of what other people will do. Stereotypes regarding the other player may influence a player to defect on the first move of the game. This is especially true if someone views another player as belonging to a group believed likely to compete. This could trigger an unending chain of competition as the other player retaliates in response to your moves. An individual will act in any situation based on his or her own perception of the environment and the expected results of whatever action might be taken, whether or not these perceptions are right. These perceptions are strongly influenced by culture and upbringing, and this viewpoint molds how individuals anticipate the likely reactions of others.

How did working as a team rather than as an individual affect your choices?

Being part of a team may make it difficult for individuals to reconcile their own interests and values with those of other group members. Many people are motivated to contribute to a group effort if they believe that the activity is honest and useful. Closely related to this is the expectation of how they will be regarded by the rest of the collective group ("community") for their actions. However, this powerful influence fades as the community becomes larger and the individual's actions become less known. In ethical terms, group size and anonymity can be factors influencing the decisions made by individuals. Risk taking is generally much higher in a group because individuals can "hide" behind a shared decision.

How did things change when players were allowed to communicate with one another?

When allowed to communicate, the players acquired the ability to influence the choices made by others. This provided a way for them to plan the best means of accumulating points—as long as each party could trust the other to follow through with the agreement. One possible negative aspect of communication involves the issue of power, because force or coercion can be used to influence the actions of other players. Overall, communication is an important factor in the game, and it generally affects the likelihood that participants will cooperate. It has been shown through field and experimental research that communication is a way of increasing cooperation in social dilemmas. Placing persons in small groups where they have to talk to one another is beneficial for creating trust and collaboration. It appears that talking about common problems can help build trust.

How does this game relate to issues of cooperation and conflict resolution in the real world?

Social dilemma research, particularly in terms of the prisoner's dilemma, defines cooperation as an act that maximizes the interest of the other (as an individual or as a collective), and it defines competition ("defection") as an act that maximizes self-interest. When conflicts arise in everyday circumstances, a person generally responds in one of several different primary modes. These conflict resolution styles (avoidance, accommodation, competition, cooperation, collaboration) can be viewed as being a function of the extent to which one shows concern for others versus the extent to which one shows concern for oneself. Studies show that consistent use of accommodation by any one individual or group can cause the appearance of being weak and willing to be exploited. It is for this reason that many people adopt a competitive approach to decision making.

What ethical guidelines did you follow in making your personal decisions? Did you view any choices made by other players as being unethical? In what way did they seem unethical? How did this influence your choices going forward?

Some scenarios presented outcomes that were more personally defined for an individual, while other situations had consequences that affected a larger group or society as a whole. The amount of control that an individual has over a situation can make a difference in making ethical choices. In addition, a person's motivation to do good work or to act ethically is grounded in the expectation that there will be some sort of "reward"—whether it is internal or external. Our past history with similar situations helps us to build a particular expectancy as to outcomes and rewards.

General Applications

- Overall, what did you learn from the game?
- How is this related to your experiences in your own organizations? Give specific examples.
- How is independent success dependent on what others do? Who do you depend on for your success?
- Are these relationships generally competitive or cooperative? Why?
- Are cooperative relationships always helpful or desirable? Why or why not?
- What can we do to change competitive relationships?
- How does your organization encourage individuals to act in a manner that benefits the entire organization?
- How does the organizational incentive structure reward individualistic, self-interested behavior? Give specific examples.
- How does the reward structure compensate for group results? What impact does this have on teamwork and the choices made by individual team members?
- What about people who always "do the right thing" no matter what the consequences?

- Do individuals have a duty to consider how their actions affect others, especially when individual interests conflict with group interests? Explain your reasoning.
- Should individuals sacrifice personal interests for the sake of others? How does this relate to ethics?
- Should moral or ethical standards be compromised for the greater good? That is, does "the end justify the means"?
- In general do groups (for example, corporations) have a duty to consider how their actions affect the community or society as a whole? Why or why not? Do individuals have a similar responsibility to society? Why or why not?
- How does this game relate to the issue of ethics in general?
- Does it pay to behave unethically? Why or why not?
- Should you behave ethically because it is in your best interest to do so or because it is the right thing to do? Why?
- What ethical guidelines exist in your organization? How are they communicated?
- How are ethical choices rewarded in your organization?
- What specific actions can be taken to guide ethical behavior?

CLOSING

1. Direct participants to go to the Learning Insights section on page 21 of the workbook. Ask individuals to write three key learning points. Allow approximately five minutes for work.
2. Distribute one copy each of Handout 1 and Handout 2 to every participant. Explain that these information sheets will be used to guide the participants in creating an action plan for behavioral change.

3. Direct participants to turn to the Action Planning section on page 23. Ask individuals to read the Handouts and to commit to two actions to improve their ability to collaborate with others and two actions to help them develop a deeper ethical awareness of their decisions. Allow approximately ten minutes for completing this task. Ask some volunteers to share their insights and action steps.

Learning Extensions

1. Review the content of each of the ethical dilemmas presented and discuss the consequences in detail. After forming subgroups of three to five participants, refer to Handout 2 and ask the groups to use the Basic Steps for Making an Ethical Decision to analyze one or more of the situations.
2. Select a recommended book on ethics appropriate to your organization. Assign a reading task to participants two to four weeks prior to a discussion session. At the session, ask participants to discuss the major learning points and apply them to general business situations.
3. Conduct a session in which participants identify several ongoing ethical situations occurring in the organization. Distribute newsprint sheets and markers to subgroups of three to five participants. Assign one issue to each group and ask them to identify the driving forces and stakeholders involved in the issue. Ask the groups to think of ways to resolve the ethical conflicts.
4. Obtain several famous quotes regarding ethics or select one of Aesop's fables that explores a particular ethical issue. Assign participants to subgroups for a discussion on how the example applies to general situations or to specific conditions within the participants' organization.
5. Assign the reading of Cliffs Notes on the book *Crime and Punishment.* Conduct a discussion session on the issue of compromising moral or ethical standards for what is to be considered the good of society.

Handout 1: Collaboration

What roles do competition and cooperation play in business and social interactions? How do the actions of an individual affect the group as a whole? Why is trust such an important factor in how we interact with others? It is important to understand the underlying psychology of these concepts in order to make appropriate personal decisions and move toward collaboration.

COMPETITION

Bombarded by constant change, organizations are facing the realities presented by the complex, competing, and contradictory demands of both internal and external environments. Competitiveness is practically guaranteed in an environment marked by increased product obsolescence, limited resources, free trade, the pursuit of greater productivity, and unstable economic conditions. Remaining competitive and keeping pace with other groups is a generally accepted condition for continued growth and prosperity in most organizations. Competition is complex—sometimes good, sometimes bad, and sometimes in between. Competition has its place in the world when it is used to motivate people to maximize their contributions in a group effort, but not at the expense of the interest of others.

COOPERATION

To gain an edge in today's highly competitive world, many organizations have turned to work teams. When discussing teamwork, most people can immediately grasp the need for cooperation among group members. In effective teams, cooperation *is* the underlying way that people work. They have a cooperative culture that signals to everyone that they are in this together and that they help each other accomplish their goals. This cooperative culture can be very productive and useful. However, a cooperative culture does not rule out a certain amount of competition and independence. The individual efforts of team members combine to produce results in a cooperative team.

COMPETITION VS. COOPERATION

There are times, however, when competition is inevitable, for example, when two or more people compete for the same job. It is important that competing parties keep sight of the short- and long-term implications of their competitive behavior, both for themselves and for others. In numerous studies that have been done to determine whether competition is better than cooperation, it was found that aggressive, "winner take all" competition typically results in less creativity, poorer performance, and reduced satisfaction. But we cannot really believe that all forms of competition—for example, a war and a game of chess—are psychologically and situationally the same. People respond to extreme competitive conditions, in which there are big gaps between winners and losers, very differently than the way they respond to moderate or minor competition, where the gap is small. When gaps between winners and losers are so large that the losers cannot envision that they can be bridged, the possibility for friendly rivalry disappears.

ROLE OF TRUST

For people who continuously compete rather than cooperate with others, the question of building a reputation of trust comes into play. If people continue to compete when given multiple opportunities for cooperation, others may not trust them, and so they may not receive the same benefits of cooperative interactions in the future. If people are by nature both trusting and trustworthy, that general altruistic concern for the well-being of others may provide sufficient reason to cooperate and keep their agreements. Habitual honesty leads to trust, and trust leads to other good things.

COLLABORATION

When the efforts of two or more individuals combine to produce an outcome that is greater than the sum of all its parts, synergy occurs. However, synergy usually only gets its full power after a long-term process of mutual cooperation. Collaboration requires mutual cooperation, and it is vital in situations that require group members to work together to produce an integrated joint effort, such as that found in teamwork. It integrates and builds on the mutual interests of all members of a group, and it simultaneously shows concern for both getting the job done and for maintaining ongoing relationships. Collaboration is probably the most difficult but potentially rewarding approach to resolving conflict situations.

CO-OPETITION

We can ask then, What relationship do cooperation and competition (and trust) have with the psychology of moral development? Most moral dilemmas involve people who want incompatible ends, or present situations in which what an individual wants is in conflict with the maintenance of a good social system. Competition can have a place in the world when it is used to motivate people to maximize their contributions in a group effort, but not at the expense of the interest of others, including society as a whole.

Strategic planners in organizations of the future need to consider the potential benefits of collaborating, cooperating, and coordinating with others who serve the same markets, rather than pursuing conventional competition. This new mindset can be described as "co-opetition." This unique approach allows for the ever-shifting alliances and partnerships that embrace competition and cooperation at the same time.

Handout 2: Ethics

Because ethics is an inexact system of individual, organizational, and societal values, beliefs, attitudes, and behaviors, many issues are not clearly black and white but various shades of gray. Ethical dilemmas naturally exist when a choice potentially conflicts with a law, adopted policy, or code of conduct, or when the choice embarrasses the individual or company. However, ethical conflicts also arise when individual interests conflict with those of others, especially the group of which the individual is a close part.

ETHICAL STANDARDS

Most people have a common-sense understanding of an ethical act as something judged proper or acceptable on some standard of right and wrong. However, ethical standards are considered part of a person's personality and are susceptible to change. There is no absolute right or wrong answer to every situation, and each individual reacts differently to ethical problems. Ethical behavior can be viewed as a "moving target" as an individual reacts to the environment and to the occasion. Although people have different morals and standards of right and wrong, many are shared by most members of society.

Ethical considerations are closely related to personal virtues of trust, integrity, and respect. If these qualities are lacking in role models, leaders, or those with whom we identify, there can be a strong influence to follow suit. Therefore, some individuals may behave unethically when they see others are doing so. This is especially true if the unethical behavior is rewarded or immune from punishment. On the opposite end of the scale, there are those who always will choose to do the "right thing" no matter what.

BUSINESS ETHICS

To many, business ethics is an oxymoron. Numerous organizations are facing legal actions resulting from decisions that were made without regard for ethical considerations. It has become more generally expected that unethical employees will be penalized, so individuals are becoming more aware of the consequences of unethical behavior. However, we often rationalize our decisions rather than explore all the possibilities for creating an ethical playing field.

One reason that making ethical choices in business is so often troublesome is that business ethics is not simply an extension of an individual's personal ethics. Having high ethical standards may not be enough to handle the tough choices that frequently arise in the workplace. Sometimes, an organization's hierarchy or the incentives created by some organizational structures can lead to ethical dilemmas. The values and ethics modeled by superiors have a strong influence on a subordinate's decision-making process.

This is also a time when many organizations are embracing "risk taking" in their pursuit to thrive, prosper, and grow. Ethics training and ethical guidelines benefit organizations by steering employees away from questionable risk taking and into more productive and appropriate kinds of risk taking that promote innovation and initiative.

ETHICAL DECISION MAKING

Making ethical choices can be a difficult and complex process, and it is not always obvious or even easy to identify the right choice. Identifying ethical behaviors and attitudes involves questioning, examining, and taking moral inventory of thoughts, ideas, attitudes, values, and behaviors specific to the individual. The focus should be on isolating internal beliefs and values from the external influence of family, peers, employers, and organizations.

BASIC STEPS FOR MAKING AN ETHICAL DECISION

1. Analyze the Actions
   - Without thinking about consequences, what are all the options available to you?
   - What would another person you respect do?
   - How do the actions measure up against moral principles (honesty, fairness, equality, respect, and so forth)?
   - Would any of your actions "cross the line" in terms of anything from simple decency to an important ethical principle?
   - If there is a conflict between principles or the rights of others, is one principle more important than the others?
   - Which option offers an action that is least problematic?
2. Analyze the Consequences
   - How would you define the problem if you stood on the other side of the fence?
   - How does the purpose of this decision compare to the probable results?
   - Who will be helped by what you do?
   - Who will be harmed?
   - What is the extent of the benefit and harm involved?
   - What are the short-term consequences?
   - What are the long-term consequences?
3. Make a Decision
   - Take both parts of your analysis into account and make your decision.

Source: Adapted from *Resolving an ethical dilemma*. Center for Ethics and Business at Loyola Marymount University. Available: www.ethicsandbusiness.org/strategy.htm

Response Cards Sheet

A	B
A	B
A	B
A	B

Bibliography

Axelrod, R. (1984). *The evolution of cooperation*. New York: Basic Books.

Brehms, B. (1996). Chaos, cheating, and cooperation: Potential solutions to the prisoner's dilemma. *OIKOS*, *76*, 14–24.

Crawford, S. (n.d.) The prisoner's dilemma in detail. *The Open University*. Available: http://open2.net/historyandhearts/philosophy_ethics/dilemma_in_detail_p.html.

Ferrell, O.C., & Gardiner, G. (1991). *In pursuit of ethics*. Springfield, IL: Smith Collins.

James, H.S. (1998). Using the prisoner's dilemma to teach business ethics when personal and group interests conflict. *Teaching Business Ethics*, *2*, 211–222.

James, H.S., Jr., & Cohen, J.P. (2004). Does ethics training neutralize the incentives of the prisoner's dilemma? Evidence from a classroom experiment. *Journal of Business Ethics*, *50*, 53–61.

Kuhn, S. (2003, August 11). Prisoner's dilemma. *Stanford encyclopedia of philosophy*. Available: http://plato.stanford.edu/entries/prisoner-dilemma

O'Donnell, M.J. (1998, Fall). The three-player prisoner's dilemma. Available: www.classes.cs.uchicago.edu/archive/1998/fall/CS105/Project/node6.html

The prisoner's dilemma in business. (1995, September). *The ethical spectacle*. Available: www.spectacle.org/995/index.html

About the Author

Lorraine Ukens, owner of Team-ing With Success (www.team-ing.com), is a performance improvement consultant who specializes in team building and experiential learning. Her business experience has been applied in designing, facilitating, and evaluating programs in a variety of areas. She has teamed with private companies, nonprofit organizations, and government agencies to help achieve higher levels of success.

Lorraine is the author of several training activity resources that make learning interactive and fun. These include activity books (*Getting Together*; *Working Together*; *All Together Now*; *Energize Your Audience*; *The New Encyclopedia of Group Activities*; *101 Ways to Improve Customer Service*; *SkillBuilders: 50 Customer Service Activities*; *Pump Them Up*), consensus simulations (*Adventure in the Amazon, Stranded in the Himalayas, Arctic Expedition, Trouble on the Inca Trail, Lost in the Cradle of Gold*), and a training game (*Common Currency: The Cooperative-Competition Game*). She is the editor of *What Smart Trainers Know: The Secrets of Success from the World's Foremost Experts*, for which she wrote a chapter on team training. She also has contributed chapters to a variety of edited books, ranging from team building to orientation.

Lorraine earned a bachelor's degree in psychology and a master's degree in human resource development from Towson University near Baltimore, Maryland. She was an adjunct faculty member in the graduate division at Towson for eight years before moving to central Florida. She served as president of the Maryland Chapter of ASTD from 1999–2000 and continues to be active in the field of training and development.

Pfeiffer Publications Guide

This guide is designed to familiarize you with the various types of Pfeiffer publications. The formats section describes the various types of products that we publish; the methodologies section describes the many different ways that content might be provided within a product. We also provide a list of the topic areas in which we publish.

FORMATS

In addition to its extensive book-publishing program, Pfeiffer offers content in an array of formats, from fieldbooks for the practitioner to complete, ready-to-use training packages that support group learning.

FIELDBOOK Designed to provide information and guidance to practitioners in the midst of action. Most fieldbooks are companions to another, sometimes earlier, work, from which its ideas are derived; the fieldbook makes practical what was theoretical in the original text. Fieldbooks can certainly be read from cover to cover. More likely, though, you'll find yourself bouncing around following a particular theme, or dipping in as the mood, and the situation, dictate.

HANDBOOK A contributed volume of work on a single topic, comprising an eclectic mix of ideas, case studies, and best practices sourced by practitioners and experts in the field.

An editor or team of editors usually is appointed to seek out contributors and to evaluate content for relevance to the topic. Think of a handbook not as a ready-to-eat meal, but as a cookbook of ingredients that enables you to create the most fitting experience for the occasion.

RESOURCE Materials designed to support group learning. They come in many forms: a complete, ready-to-use exercise (such as a game); a comprehensive resource on one topic (such as conflict management) containing a variety of methods and approaches; or a collection of like-minded activities (such as icebreakers) on multiple subjects and situations.

TRAINING PACKAGE An entire, ready-to-use learning program that focuses on a particular topic or skill. All packages comprise a guide for the facilitator/trainer and a workbook for the participants. Some packages are supported with additional media—such as video—or learning aids, instruments, or other devices to help participants understand concepts or practice and develop skills.

- *Facilitator/trainer's guide* Contains an introduction to the program, advice on how to organize and facilitate the learning event, and step-by-step instructor notes. The guide also contains copies of presentation materials—handouts, presentations, and overhead designs, for example—used in the program.
- *Participant's workbook* Contains exercises and reading materials that support the learning goal and serves as a valuable reference and support guide for participants in the weeks and months that follow the learning event. Typically, each participant will require his or her own workbook.

ELECTRONIC CD-ROMs and web-based products transform static Pfeiffer content into dynamic, interactive experiences. Designed to take advantage of the searchability, automation, and ease-of-use that technology provides, our e-products bring convenience and immediate accessibility to your workspace.

METHODOLOGIES

CASE STUDY A presentation, in narrative form, of an actual event that has occurred inside an organization. Case studies are not prescriptive, nor are they used to prove a point; they are designed to develop critical analysis and decision-making skills. A case study has a specific time frame, specifies a sequence of events, is narrative in structure, and contains a plot structure—an issue (what should be/have been done?). Use case studies when the goal is to enable participants to apply previously learned theories to the circumstances in the case, decide what is pertinent, identify the real issues, decide what should have been done, and develop a plan of action.

ENERGIZER A short activity that develops readiness for the next session or learning event. Energizers are most commonly used after a break or lunch to stimulate or refocus the group. Many involve some form of physical activity, so they are a useful way to counter post-lunch lethargy. Other uses include transitioning from one topic to another, where "mental" distancing is important.

EXPERIENTIAL LEARNING ACTIVITY (ELA) A facilitator-led intervention that moves participants through the learning cycle from experience to application (also known as a Structured Experience). ELAs are carefully thought-out designs in which there is a definite learning purpose and intended outcome. Each step—everything that participants do during the activity—facilitates the accomplishment of the stated goal. Each ELA includes complete instructions for facilitating the intervention and a clear statement of goals, suggested group size and timing, materials required, an explanation of the process, and, where appropriate, possible variations to the activity. (For more detail on Experiential Learning Activities, see the Introduction to the *Reference Guide to Handbooks and Annuals*, 1999 edition, Pfeiffer, San Francisco.)

GAME A group activity that has the purpose of fostering team spirit and togetherness in addition to the achievement of a pre-stated goal. Usually contrived—undertaking a desert expedition, for example—this type of learning method offers an engaging means for participants to demonstrate and practice business and interpersonal skills. Games are effective for team building and personal development mainly because the goal is subordinate to the process—the means through which participants reach decisions, collaborate, communicate, and generate trust and understanding. Games often engage teams in "friendly" competition.

ICEBREAKER A (usually) short activity designed to help participants overcome initial anxiety in a training session and/or to acquaint the participants with one another. An icebreaker can be a fun activity or can be tied to specific topics or training goals. While a useful tool in itself, the icebreaker comes into its own in situations where tension or resistance exists within a group.

INSTRUMENT A device used to assess, appraise, evaluate, describe, classify, and summarize various aspects of human behavior. The term used to describe an instrument depends primarily on its format and purpose. These terms include survey, questionnaire, inventory, diagnostic, survey, and poll. Some uses of instruments include providing instrumental feedback to group members, studying here-and-now processes or functioning within a group, manipulating group composition, and evaluating outcomes of training and other interventions.

Instruments are popular in the training and HR field because, in general, more growth can occur if an individual is provided with a method for focusing specifically on his or her own behavior. Instruments also are used to obtain information that will serve as a basis for change and to assist in workforce planning efforts.

Paper-and-pencil tests still dominate the instrument landscape with a typical package comprising a facilitator's guide, which offers advice on administering the instrument and interpreting the collected data, and an initial set of instruments. Additional instruments are available separately. Pfeiffer, though, is investing heavily in e-instruments. Electronic instrumentation provides effortless distribution and, for larger groups particularly, offers advantages over paper-and-pencil tests in the time it takes to analyze data and provide feedback.

LECTURETTE A short talk that provides an explanation of a principle, model, or process that is pertinent to the participants' current learning needs. A lecturette is intended to establish a common language bond between the trainer and the participants by providing a mutual frame of reference. Use a lecturette as an introduction to a group activity or event, as an interjection during an event, or as a handout.

MODEL A graphic depiction of a system or process and the relationship among its elements. Models provide a frame of reference and something more tangible, and more easily remembered, than a verbal explanation. They also give participants something to "go on," enabling them to track their own progress as they experience the dynamics, processes, and relationships being depicted in the model.

ROLE PLAY A technique in which people assume a role in a situation/scenario: a customer service rep in an angry-customer exchange, for example. The way in which the role is approached is then discussed and feedback is offered. The role play is often repeated using a different approach and/or incorporating changes made based on feedback received. In other words, role playing is a spontaneous interaction involving realistic behavior under artificial (and safe) conditions.

SIMULATION A methodology for understanding the interrelationships among components of a system or process. Simulations differ from games in that they test or use a model that depicts or mirrors some aspect of reality in form, if not necessarily in content. Learning occurs by studying the effects of change on one or more factors of the model. Simulations are commonly used to test hypotheses about what happens in a system—often referred to as "what if?" analysis—or to examine best-case/worst-case scenarios.

THEORY A presentation of an idea from a conjectural perspective. Theories are useful because they encourage us to examine behavior and phenomena through a different lens.

TOPICS

The twin goals of providing effective and practical solutions for workforce training and organization development and meeting the educational needs of training and human resource professionals shape Pfeiffer's publishing program. Core topics include the following:

Leadership & Management
Communication & Presentation
Coaching & Mentoring
Training & Development
E-Learning
Teams & Collaboration
OD & Strategic Planning
Human Resources
Consulting